SAFFRON WALDEN & AROUND

THROUGH TIME

Kate J. Cole

AMBERLEY

Bridge End Gardens, Easter 2015

First published 2015

Amberley Publishing
The Hill, Stroud
Gloucestershire, GL5 4EP

www.amberley-books.com

Copyright © Kate J. Cole , 2015

The right of Kate J. Cole to be identified as
the Author of this work has been asserted in
accordance with the Copyrights, Designs and
Patents Act 1988.

ISBN 978-1-4456-4493-6 (print)
ISBN 978-1-4456-4513-1 (ebook)

British Library Cataloguing in Publication Data.
A catalogue record for this book is available from
the British Library.

Typeset in 9.5pt on 12pt Celeste.
Typesetting by Amberley Publishing.
Printed in the UK.

Contents

Introduction

Each year, the Halifax Bank commissions a study to discover the best rural place to live in Britain. In spring 2014, the award of *Rural Areas Quality of Life Survey* went to the north-west Essex district of Uttlesford. The district was judged on its residents' quality of life; including health, employment, schooling and general standard of living. Uttlesford was found to have the highest standard of living in rural Britain.

For those who live in Uttlesford (or once lived in the area) the study's findings come as no surprise. With villages full of pargeted houses painted in bright colours, nestling alongside thatched cottages, Uttlesford is a beautiful rural district. But, although rural in its nature, its towns and villages are fully equipped to survive modern-day living courtesy of the district's excellent road, rail and air connections.

This book's aim is to show you how some of the towns and villages within Uttlesford have evolved through time. From the beautiful town of Saffron Walden (containing three hundred and eighty-three listed buildings) to the tiny ancient villages of Audley End (with its world-renowned Jacobean mansion and a further forty-seven listed buildings), Littlebury (eighty listed buildings), Wendens Ambo (thirty-two listed buildings) and the Chesterfords (eighty-six buildings split between two villages). This is the story of some of the towns and villages within rural Uttlesford through time.

At the beginning of 2015, my family's own long connection with the district of Uttlesford came to an end when I moved from Great Dunmow to Maldon. I have swapped the rural prettiness of Uttlesford for the wild but stunning salt marshes of Essex's coast line. Two districts in Essex close to my heart, both demonstrating the diverse beauty and the rich heritage of this unique county of ours.

Kate Cole
Maldon – Summer 2015
www.essexvoicespast.com

CHAPTER 1

Saffron Walden

Market Place (Facing South, West Side), Postmarked 1905

The right to hold a market in Saffron Walden started in 1141 with the town's earliest market place located within the castle's grounds. The market moved to its current location sometime in the medieval period, although most of the trade was originally conducted in the tiny rows of shops which were once between current-day King Street and Market Row. The market's importance to the town's fortunes can be seen by the name of the town itself: for many centuries it was known as Chepying (or Chipping) Walden, 'chepying' meaning 'market'. The town only took its current form of Saffron Walden from the late sixteenth century; although some newspapers used the name Chipping Walden as recently as the first part of the nineteenth century. During the early sixteenth century, a new religious guild, Holy Trinity, with controlling civic powers, was created within the town. This led to Henry VIII granting the guild a new charter in 1514 for a market to be held in Saffron Walden, and for the guild to keep the income from the market.

Market Place (West Side) Including the Water Fountain, Postmarked 1912
Following the granting of its Charter in 1514, the market continued to thrive as an important area trading in both produce and livestock. The Market Place was also used as an area to hold civic and community celebrations such as mayoral elections, along with coronation and peace celebrations. During the nineteenth and early twentieth centuries, the market place also held regular biannual horse fairs in March and September with the fairs renowned throughout East Anglia. In 1863, George Stacey Gibson and his mother, Deborah, financed the purchase of the water fountain which is still present in Market Place. The water fountain was designed by John Francis Bentley (1839–1902) and exhibited at the International Exhibition of 1862. The Gibsons gave the fountain to the town of Saffron Walden in commemoration of the 1863 wedding of Prince Albert Edward (the Prince of Wales) to Princess Alexandra of Denmark (later King Edward VII and Queen Alexandra).

Corn Exchange, Shortly after It was Built in 1848

On the 6 July 1848, the foundation stone for the new Corn Exchange was laid by Saffron Walden's Mayor Joseph L. Taylor and Alderman Wyatt George Gibson in front of a large audience from the town. The Corn Exchange, designed by the architect Richard Tress of London, had eighteen corn merchants' offices, a committee room, and a public reading room. The opening in the centre of the building was twenty-five feet by thirty-five feet. The Corn Exchange was privately financed via shareholders and private subscribers at a cost of £2,500. A medieval timber framed building, the Woolcombers guildhall, had previously stood in the same location. Eighty-five men, under the control of the builder Charles Erswell, were continuously on site during the demolition of the old guildhall and the building of the new Corn Exchange. After the formal ceremony at the laying of the foundation stone, the mayor entertained the local dignitaries at his house, whilst all eighty-five workers were treated to a feast of 'Old English Fare' at the home of the builder. *Inset:* Artistic impression of the Woolcombers' guildhall in the Market Place before the 1840s.

Election of the Mayor, Market Place, Postmarked 1904

The mock-Tudor front to the Town Hall, seen today in Market Place, was built in 1879, financed by George Stacey Gibson. The façade was placed on the original Georgian Town Hall, which had been built in 1761 on the site of a Tudor guildhall of the Holy Trinity. The Georgian Town Hall had a lock-up gaol on the ground floor, facing into the Market Place. The gaol was removed in 1818 and rebuilt as a new house of correction at the cost of £400, near to the Workhouse at the top of the High Street (then known as Cuckingstool End Street). The same year, as part of the general improvements to Market Place, the town's Market Cross, the pillory, the whipping post and the stocks were also removed. The improvements to Market Place was partially financed by public subscription. *Inset:* Date plaque from when the Town Hall's mock-Tudor façade was built.

Market Square (Facing East, South Side), Postmarked 1905

The elaborate Victorian building on the left side of the images was built in 1874 by local philanthropist and Quaker, George Stacey Gibson (1818–1883) for his private bank, the Gibson Tuke & Gibson bank (originally known as the Saffron Walden and North Essex bank which opened in the town in 1824). In 1896, the bank (along with nineteen other small private banks) was amalgamated to form Barclays Bank. Tuke was Gibson's brother-in-law, William Murray Tuke, and his arrival as a partner at Gibson's Saffron Walden bank in 1863 started a long connection between the Tuke family and Barclays Bank. This only ended in 2001 with the death of Sir Anthony Tuke, chairman of Barclays Bank (as was Sir Anthony's father and grandfather) who was William Murray Tuke's great-grandson. Even today, nearly one hundred and fifty years after it was built, the building in Saffron Walden is still a branch of Barclays Bank. *Inset:* £20 banknote from Gibson, Tuke & Gibson bank.

Coronation Day, Market Place, 22 June 1911

On 22 June 1911, Edward VII's second son was crowned King George V. Towns and villages throughout Great Britain celebrated his coronation by holding street parties and community festivities. Celebrations started in Saffron Walden on Coronation Day by the church ringing out a Coronation peal at 7.00 a.m. At 10.30 a.m., the Mayor's procession assembled in the Market Square ready to walk to the church for an 11.00 a.m. service. At 11.45 a.m., an 'address of congratulations' was read out in the market place (this is the event taking place in the top postcard). Then there was a distribution of coronation medals to the children, and the national anthem was sung. In the afternoon, there was a dinner for the old people of the town in the town hall, and a cricket match was played on the common. The bottom photograph shows the lady dignitaries of the town (on the right) and groups of school children (on the left). It is sad to realise that many of the schoolboys shown in the bottom photograph probably died a few years later during the First World War. (Bottom postcard reproduced courtesy of Jean Harrison)

Market Place, 1919

In November 1919, the people of Saffron Walden and surrounding villages came together in the Market Place to commemorate the armistice at the end of the First World War, a war which had claimed the lives of so many of their own. As the war progressed, the town's casualities were enscribed onto the Roll of Honour kept in the Market Place, propped up on Deborah and George Stacey Gibson's Victorian water fountain. The eventual number of the town's dead was 159 men. During that first Armistice Day, a German field gun, captured by the Essex Regiment, was displayed in the Market Place. The town also celebrated the peace earlier in the summer of the same year, after the conferences in Versailles in June 1919 had resulted in the signing of various peace treaties. To celebrate the peace, the town raised approximately £600 for local celebrations. On Saturday 19 July 1919, there was a procession of demobilised or discharged soldiers, sailors and airmen who marched from the Common to Market Place. A dinner for 400 people, consisting of roast beef, plum pudding and beer, was held in the Town Hall and Corn Exchange. In the afternoon, there were sports on the Common for all the children and evening tea at all the schools. In the evening, a grand procession wove its way through town headed by the town's band. The day finished with a two-thousand-candle arc lamp lit on top of the Debden Road's water tower, with fireworks and a bonfire on the Common, where an effigy of Kaiser Wilhelm II was burnt. Afterwards, the town went home to quietly mourn their dead. (Top postcard reproduced courtesy of Jean Harrison. Bottom postcard reproduced courtesy of Robina Veal)

Rose & Crown and Town Hall, Market Place, c. 1900s

In the background of the Edwardian photograph (behind the water fountain) is the Rose & Crown pub. In the early hours of Boxing Day 1969, the Rose & Crown was destroyed by fire which had swept through the building. The fire killed eleven people. A further seventeen people had to be rescued by fireman and members of the public. All had been staying in the hotel over Christmas. The fire was devastating: seventy-five firemen from ten stations with twelve appliances (including five pumps) attended the fire. Afterwards, it was found that there were several contributing factors which led to the severity of the fire. The tragedy directly led to the government issuing a major piece of British legislation, the 1971 Fire Precautions Act. From this time onwards, amongst other far-reaching safety measures, hotels have had to comply with fire safety regulations and be inspected for Fire Certificates. Today, people who were living Saffron Walden in 1969, or who have family who were in the fire service in attendance, still vividly recall the horror and despair of that night. The only reminders to modern shoppers that Boots was once the Rose & Crown, are the hotel's original bunch of hops now hanging over Boots' entrance, the shell canopy set in the wall of the alley, and the name of the alleyway. *Inset:* The Rose & Crown's bunch of hops.

Market Hill, Saffron Walden   Guy Saffron Walden

Market Hill (Facing Church Street), Postmarked 1906

Before the nineteenth century this road was known as Market End. The building on the left was constructed from 1854 to 1855 for John Leverett (1793–1859), a draper and grocer who was also the mayor of Saffron Walden in 1851 and an alderman throughout the 1850s. The earliest photographs of Saffron Walden market place (dated 1854/1855) show that Leverett had been the agent for the Royal Exchange Assurance Corporation from at least that time. The Edwardian postcard demonstrates that Leverett's in Market Hill were still the local agent for the Royal Exchange, even fifty years after John Leverett's death. After Leverett's death, his son, Stebbing Leverett (1836–1909) took over his shop. Stebbing Leverett was an alderman of the town for thirty-seven years, until his death in 1909. The tall building in the middle-left of the postcard was The Green Dragon pub. The pub closed in the 1930s when it became a saddlery and leather shop. *Inset:* 1926 advertisement for Stebbing Leverett & Son Outfitters. The Leveretts had been in Market Place since 1788. (The date of 1926 is the date of advertisement.)

1788 - 1926
STEBBING LEVERETT
& SON
Market Place, SAFFRON WALDEN
Telegrams: Leverett, Saffron Walden.   Telephone: 111.

Ladies' and Gentlemen's complete Outfitters
Hosiers & Hatters

Complete Outfitters for Saffron Walden and Newport Schools
Agents for Jaeger Pure Wool Underwear and Aertex Cellular
Day and night wear.

Market Row, Early 1920s

Before the nineteenth century, the area between King Street and Hill Street (in the north and south) and Cross Street and Market Place (in the west and east) was a cluster of small rows with market stalls and shops. The names of each row is evocative of the trade which once took place in each row: Tanners Row, Fish Row, Mercer's Row, Butcher Row, Butter Market, and Pig Street. Today, most of these ancient rows have been combined into one main name, Market Row; with the names of other rows, such as Mercer's Row and Butcher Row, still used as addresses by shops. The photograph above is of Lizzie Clayden with her son, Ken 'Casey' Clayden *c.* 1921–1922 standing in the doorway of Lizzie's house at No. 10 Market Row. (Postcard reproduced courtesy of Robina Veal)

King Street, Saffron Walden

King Street (Facing Towards the High Street), Postmarked 1906

The first shop on the left was Francis John Taylor's Cyclists Rest and Victorian café; next door is David Barton's tailors, millinery and drapery shop. In the centre of the picture, on the corner of Market Passage, is the fishmongers and poultry shop of Frank Hardwick (now a butcher's shop). In January 1919, the Victorian Café hosted a dinner for twenty-three Saffron Walden men who had returned from Germany after being prisoners of war during the First World War. Members of the town council were present, and after the meal, the repatriated soldiers went to the Town Hall where they were received by the Mayor and Mayoress. *Inset:* 1926 advert for Frank Hardwick's fishmongers.

David Barton & Son, King Street, Postmarked 1907

The Edwardian photograph is a composite postcard showing David Barton's two tailors, drapery and millinery shops, both in King Street. On the right-hand side is his original shop, on the corner of King Street and Market Passage (now No. 7 King Street). The left image is his other shop, three doors away nearer the market (now No. 1 King Street). The red tiling and distinctive windows on both shops (still present today) were placed on the buildings *c.* 1900. David Barton kept a millinery, drapery and tailor's shop in King Street from around the 1860s until his death in 1922. Before him, during the nineteenth century his father, James Barton, also kept a tailor's shop first in Hill Street and then in Market Place, and finally in Market Street. *Inset:* 1889 advertisement for D. Barton.

King Street (from the Corner of High Street), after 1920

This street has a long tradition of being one of the main commercial areas within the town of Saffron Walden. Until the late eighteenth century, from approximately present-day Market Passage to the start of the Market Place there was a small narrow row of shops in the middle of the street called Middle Row. The tiny gap between Middle Row and the south side of current-day King Street was called, appropriately, Creep Mouse Alley. The rest of current-day King Street (from the junction with the High Street, to the start of Market Place) was called Market End Street. Middle Row and Creep Mouse Alley were demolished in the 1760s. Some of the buildings in King Street date from the fifteenth and sixteenth centuries, including a large medieval hall house (currently Nos 17, 19 and 21 King Street) and smaller sixteenth century buildings at No. 13 and No. 15. *Inset:* King Street's medieval hall house.

Fire in King Street, 1908

On Thursday 30 January 1908, fire broke out in King Street in the warehouses of J. J. Robson & Sons, wholesale and retail merchants and grocers. The town's fire brigade was called, and was quickly on the scene. They were able to put out the flames in the warehouses (which was totally gutted) and the retail shop had extensive water damage. The damage was estimated at between £4,000 and £5,000. A further fire took place in the next-door premises a few weeks later on Wednesday 4 March 1908. The premises of Gayford and Woodward (auctioneers), Bonheur and Whitehead (solicitors) and the London Central Meat Company, all on the south side of King Street, were destroyed. This fire was so intense that shops on the north side of King Street were damaged by the heat and glass in their windows shattered. This second fire was more serious than the first, and during the blaze, all the buildings on both sides of the road (including the Cross Keys Hotel) from approximately the location of the modern-day Central Arcade to the junction with the High Street were thought to be at risk; but fortunately only the south side was affected. This second fire caused at least £2,000 worth of damage. These two disastrous fires account for the relatively modern buildings along this part of King Street. (Postcard reproduced courtesy of Jean Harrison)

Cross Keys Inn, High Street, after 1920

Part of the Cross Keys Inn was built in the late fourteenth century and is a timber-framed building which was formerly a medieval/Tudor house and shops. During the nineteenth century, the roof was raised to its current height, and in common with many other old inns, its timber frame was plastered over. This plaster was removed in 1920 to reveal its original timbers. In 1826, an advertisement for the sale of the inn described it as having,

> two parlours, kitchens, tap-room, bar, large market room, dining room upstairs, several excellent bedrooms, capital ale cellar, capable of stowing considerable quantity of beer, detached wine and liquor cellars, large yard, stabling for horses, several out-houses, one which was formerly brew-house, new-erected pan-tiled cart-shed, etc. The inn has been for many years most excellent market-house, persons usually dining on Saturday, very much frequented by the inhabitants, and has the advantage of two respectable benefit clubs. The beer and liquor trade is considerable, and it well-known that occupiers have invariably realized large sums of money.

Dorset House and Church Path, Church Street, *c.* 1920s

The brick building on the right side of the postcard was Dorset House, but was demolished in 1958 and in its place was planted a very pleasant garden which was renovated by the Town Council in 2011. The iron railings and gate leading into the churchyard were removed during the Second World War and melted down as part of the town's war effort. The buildings on the left were built in the fifteenth century with substantial modifications made in the nineteenth and twentieth century. *Inset:* The modern-day sculpture in Dorset House Gardens is entitled 'Walden Family' by Val Bunn.

2242. CHURCH TOWER, S., SAFFRON WALDEN.

St Mary the Virgin Church, Early 1900s

St Mary the Virgin, is the largest church in Essex. It was built in the mid-thirteenth century but there was probably a church present in the town since Saxon times. The church as seen today is the consequence of rebuilding work which took place between 1450 and 1525 under the guidance of two master masons, who also worked on Eton and King's College Chapel. By the late eighteenth century, the church had become so run-down and near derelict that it was closed for public services as the structure was unsafe. The church was restored between 1790 and 1793, and the spire was added in 1831 replacing an earlier lead-covered timber lanthorn. The church was restored again during the period 1859 to 1860, and part of the works undertaken at this time included the sealing of the vault containing the remains of ten Earls of Suffolk of Audley End, and 1st Lord Braybrooke and his two wives.

St Mary the Virgin's Churchyard, Early 1900s

According to the surviving burial registers of St Mary's, which start in 1558, there have been 780 burials inside the church. As there are no surviving records prior to 1558, it is unknown how many earlier burials took place inside the church. Those buried within the confines of a church's walls would be local gentry, successful tradesmen, the elite and wealthy townsfolk. The rest of the parish would be buried in the churchyard which has resulted in many thousands of graves and tombs at St Mary's. In common with many mid-nineteenth century large parish churchyards throughout England, St Mary's churchyard had become full to overflowing so was closed for burials in 1857. However, a further eighteen burials took place in the years up to 1892. Since 1892, the only burials in St Mary's has been for Lord and Lady Butler of Saffron Walden (the former in 1982 and the latter in 2009).

Church Walk, c. 1900s

On the left side of these images are the Verger's Cottage (in the foreground) and the Parish Room (fading into the distance). The Verger's Cottage dates from around the late fifteenth/early sixteenth century, before the English Reformation when the building was likely to be used by the parish priests in their preparations for Mass. The Parish Room was built in the Victorian period in the late nineteenth century, but was built to match the earlier Verger's Cottage. The buildings were modernised in the early 1990s.

Sun Inn, Church Street, Early 1900s

This cluster of buildings, on the corner of Market Hill and Church Street, date from the fourteenth and fifteenth centuries, with the plaster and pargetting added in the seventeenth century. In 1647, at the end of the English Civil War, the Sun Inn was the headquarters of the New Model Army, under the command of General Thomas Fairfax (1612–1671). Under orders from Parliament, Oliver Cromwell (1599–1658) and three other officer-MPs visited the army at Saffron Walden. The army were in conflict with Parliament over pay and conditions of their discharge, and the four men were sent by Parliament to negotiate a settlement with them. Cromwell stayed at the Inn from 2 to 19 May 1647 but left the town without reaching a settlement with the army. Shortly afterwards, the army left Saffron Walden when the army marched from the town to Newmarket. *Inset:* Pargeting on the Sun Inn, thought to be either Thomas Hickathrift and the Wisbech Giant or Gog and Magog.

The Museum, Postmarked 1906

Saffron Walden museum, in the shadow of Walden's castle (visible in the Edwardian postcard), is one of Britain's oldest museums and was purpose-built by the town's Natural History Society. The museum was opened in May 1835, financed by subscriptions and donations, and built on land owned by Lord Braybrooke. It also housed the meeting rooms for the Agricultural Society until 1879, after which time the Agricultural Society moved into the newly renovated Town Hall. The museum was originally run by trustees and a board of management. Visiting the museum was controlled, as this extract from an 1835 local newspaper demonstrates:

> The scientific and intelligent stranger will have every facility afforded him as far as is practicable, in seeing the Museum at any suitable hour; but application is to made to Trustee, or the Board of Management, for admission, which obtained most readily Tuesday in each week, the useful day admission during the summer months.

Today, the museum and collections are still owned by the original society, which is now known as Saffron Walden Museum Society. Since 1974, Uttlesford District Council has run the museum.

The Castle, Postmarked 1907

Walden Castle was built sometime between 1125 and 1141 by Geoffrey de Mandeville (died 1144) the 1st Earl of Essex and the grandson of another Geoffrey de Mandeville who had come to England with William the Conqueror. In 1143, during the civil wars between the Empress Matilda and King Stephen, Stephen arrested de Mandeville and seized all his castles, including Walden Castle. As soon as de Mandeville was released, he launched a campaign against the king, but died in battle following an injury from an arrow during the siege of Burwell Castle in Cambridgeshire. After King Stephen's death, Empress Matilda's son, Henry, became King Henry II. In 1158, on the orders of Henry II Walden Castle's defences were destroyed so that it was left unfortified. The castle continued to be inhabited for a further 100 years or so and was briefly fortified again in the 1340s. In 1796 the tower seen on the left side of the images was built. Recent excavations by archaeologists discovered that most of the foundations of the castle are missing, and were probably looted by people for their houses and buildings.

Castle Street (Facing Towards the High Street), Early 1900s

The pretty, colourful cottages in Castle Street, running along the side St Mary's parish church, once housed some of the poorest members of Saffron Walden's town. Census returns for 1851 shows that this street was inhabited mainly by agricultural labourers and labourers, but also residents such as tradesmen such as a coopers, tanners, painters, bakers, carpenters, warehousemen, blacksmith, and tailors. Almost in the centre of the postcard is a gabled building (at the left edge of the modern photo). This is Bellingham Buildings, a group of almshouses, now private houses, built in 1879 by the Trustees of the Amalgamated Charities of Saffron Walden. Prior to the building of the almhouses, a large maltings was in situ at this location. In the 1930s, the town cleared some of the slums in the Castle Street, including slums around the area in the street known as Sarah's Place. Today it is one of the town's most desirable roads to live in. (Postcard reproduced courtesy of Jane Fairweather)

Our Lady of Compassion Catholic Church, Castle Street, Postmarked 1908

The Catholic Church, in Castle Street, was opened in 1906. The building was converted from a sixteenth-century barn which had once belonged to The Close. Revd Father C. F. Norgate (whose photograph is inset into the above postcard) was one of the six original priests from the Catholic Missionaries of Our Lady of Compassion who had purchased the barn. In the initial days of the church, it was so popular that by June 1906 there were reports in local newspapers that there was not enough room in the church so the priests had to use a temporary church elsewhere in Castle Street. The modern-day photograph is the outside of the Catholic Church, in the shadow of the Church of England's St Mary's church which was, of course, the town's Catholic Church during the medieval era and part of the Tudor period.

Dutch Gardens, Saffron Walden.

Bridge End Gardens, Castle Street, Postmarked 1904

Also known as Fry's Garden, Bridge End Garden, one of Saffron Walden's hidden treasures, was created in the 1840s by Francis Gibson (1805–1858). Gibson, a keen landscape gardener, created his garden from a smaller garden created by his father, Atkinson Francis Gibson (1763–1829). After Francis Gibson's death, the gardens were inherited by the Fry family, who still own the gardens but in recent years have leased them to Saffron Walden Town Council. By the late twentieth century, the gardens had become overgrown and unkempt, but a major restoration programme in the 2000s has recaptured the gardens and restored them into beautiful Victorian gardens for all to use. The gardens are a series of linked areas, each with a different design and theme. The postcard above shows the Dutch Garden; other gardens include the Rose Garden, The Wilderness, the Summerhouse Lawn, the Walled Garden and the Hedge Maze. *Inset:* Tucked away between houses on Castle Street is this house with the entrance into Bridge End Gardens.

Saffron Walden   *Windmill Hill*

Windmill Hill, Early 1900s

A classic view of Saffron Walden is when driving from the top of Windmill Hill and slowing down to navigate through the narrow road at the bottom and step bend on into Bridge Street and the town. Today, the road still has a relatively steep descent, but it is likely that the hill was higher in the past. In 1826, a Cambridge newspaper reported that, 'The inhabitants of Saffron Walden have lately been at a great expense in lowering and improving Windmill Hill, on the north side of the town.' The Eight Bells pub (seen just behind the car in the modern photo) was built during the fifteenth and sixteenth centuries. The licence for the Eight Bells was originally held by a pub in Hill Street, which was demolished when the Borough Market was built in 1831.

Bridge Street (Facing away from Town), Early 1900s

In 1849, one of Essex's most notorious unsolved murders took place in Bridge Street. The victim was William Campling, the Chief Constable and Borough Surveyor of Saffron Walden. He died on 9 November 1849, aged fifty-three, some nine days after he had been shot in the legs. At his inquest, Campling's neighbour, Mary Brewer, stated that she was upstairs with Miss Campling and saw him come home after he'd been at the Eight Bells pub. They heard a gunshot and found Campling downstairs lying by the front door. Several other witnesses all heard the gunshot and Campling cry out 'I'm shot, I'm shot', but no one witnessed the shooting. Campling received at least sixty shots from a shotgun to his right leg and forty shots to his left leg. He died nine days later, in tremendous pain, from gangrene and shock. The chief suspect was Benjamin Pettit, a painter aged twenty-one, who had fallen out with Campling some months earlier. Before he died, Campling gave a statement in front of Pettit and Mayor Nathaniel Catlin, stating:

> [Pettit] had threatened me at other times: the last time I heard him threaten me was when I met him in the passage down by the Abbey Lane Chapel, in Saffron Walden; I should think it must be three or four months ago: I met him on a sudden; I think his expression was in a sort of wrath 'You old you *****, I'll do your business for you one of these times.'

At Pettit's trial in Chelmsford at the assizes of March 1850, despite plenty of circumstantial evidence indicating that he was the murderer, he was found not guilty. *Inset:* Memorial to William Campling on the wall next to the entrance to Bridge End Gardens.

Bridge Street (Facing away from Town), *c.* **1934**

On the left side of the pictures is the end of No. 1 Myddleton Place, one of the town's finest medieval buildings. It was built at the end of the fifteenth century as a merchant's house and later converted during the eighteenth and nineteenth centuries into maltings. It is believed to be the town's oldest building and is one of the most photographed buildings in Essex. From the late 1940s until 2011, the house was owned by the Youth Hostel Association, and was laid out with dormitories. After the sale to a private purchaser in 2011, the house was extensively renovated, restored and converted into residential use. *Inset:* No. 1 Myddleton Place with its maltings' hoist.

Voluntary Aid Detachment Hospital, Walden Place, 1918

Walden Place (known as Hogg's Green in the mid-nineteenth century census returns) is a red-brick building built in the middle of the eighteenth century as a country house. In the mid-nineteenth century, it was the home of Justice of the Peace, Mayor and Alderman Nathaniel Catlin, and by the end of the century, the home of the Revd R. P. Pelly, vicar of St Mary's. During the First World War, from May 1915 until April 1919, Walden Place became a Voluntary Aid Detachment (VAD) Hospital. Throughout this time, it treated injured and sick soldiers from all over Britain. It was run by forty-three qualified nurses, and ten unqualified ladies, many of whom appear in the many group photographs which exist of the hospital. More than a thousand men were treated at the hospital, including several local men from Saffron Walden. There was only one death in the entire time the hospital was open. Since the 1980s, Walden Place has been a sheltered housing complex for the over 1960s, run by Uttlesford District Council. (Postcard reproduced courtesy of Jane Fairweather)

Voluntary Aid Detachment Hospital, Walden Place, 1918

The tall gentleman in the back row standing in the doorway in the top photograph is John Goodwin. He was born in Castle Street in 1888 and his wife Bertha was born in East Street in 1890. They were married in St Mary's church in 1911 and had five children. One son, Eric, was killed in the Second World War and is commemorated on the town's war memorial. During the First World War, John Goodwin served with the Cambridgeshire Regiment, although he was attached to the 9th Suffolks when he was wounded. On the 5 January 1918, he appeared on casualty lists, possibly wounded by a gas shell. He arrived at the hospital in Saffron Walden sometime after his injury. After the First World War, he returned to his job at the gasworks in Thaxted Road and remained there until he retired. John and Bertha lived most of their married lives in Little Walden Road. John died in 1959 and Bertha died in 1980. The modern-day photograph is of Alan and Eileen Fairweather. Eileen is the granddaughter of John and Bertha. Alan Fairweather, who served in Great Dunmow's fire brigade, was one of the seventy-five firemen in attendance at the fire at the Rose and Crown in 1969. (Photographs reproduced courtesy of Jane Fairweather)

High Street, after 1934

The house on the right is The Close, a building which was built in the fifteenth and sixteenth centuries. From the sixteenth century until 1934, attached to it was another timber-framed house (to its right). In the mid-nineteenth century, both houses were occupied by Francis Gibson (1805–1858), brother of Wyatt George Gibson. In 1854, Francis enclosed the right-hand building in red brick to make a grand three-storey Victorian town house. The left building had already had its timber frame plastered over, possibly in the 1700s. In 1934, eighty years after the right building was entombed in brick, it was dismantled by Sir Ralph Harwood in its entirety and re-erected in West Grinstead, without its red brick. It is now known as Walden Hall, and is a magnificent Tudor country house looking as though it has been at its current location for centuries, not the mere eighty years it has been in Sussex. When the brick-clad building was taken down, part of a twelfth-century stone market cross was found to be supporting a wall in the house. The only known surviving fragment of Saffron Walden's medieval stone market cross is now in the house in Sussex. The plaster cladding on the remaining building was removed the same year. Inset: The Close.

High Street (Facing North), Coronation Day, 22 June 1911
Decorations were in abundance all around town on the day of George V's coronation. All the town's civic buildings and shops were festooned with bunting, evergreens and fairy lamps and at the junctions of the town's streets were arches made out of flowers and evergreens. In the evening, there was a procession through the town's main streets, and fireworks and dancing took place on the Common until past midnight. The building on the left was a private house and owned in the early twentieth century by Dr J. P. Atkinson, who was the mayor at the time of the 1911 coronation. His house later became the town's post office between 1920 and 1997. (Postcard reproduced courtesy of Jean Harrison)

Abbey Hotel, High Street (Looking North), 24 June 1915

On Thursday 24 June 1915, the massed bands of the Queen's Westminster Rifles, the Kensington (Princess Louise's) Battalion, the Saffron Walden Town Band, the Excelsior Band and the London Scottish Pipers gave an outdoor concert on the Common. After the concert, the London Scottish Pipers marched through some of the streets of the town, where a photographer captured them on their march down the High Street and past the Abbey Hotel. The Abbey Hotel was a temperance hotel, serving only non-alcoholic drinks (hence the Cadbury Chocolate sign on the door). On the right side of the modern-day photograph is the empty hanging bracket for the sign of the now redundant Greyhound pub. The Greyhound was the place where the town's food riots broke out in 1795.

Almshouses, Abbey Lane, Postmarked 1906

The almshouses were founded by the Guild of Our Lady of Pity in 1400 to provide housing for thirteen poor men. During the reign of the boy-king, Edward VI, the almshouses were seized by the king under the Chantries Act of 1547, but he later returned them to the town in 1549, under the condition that they were known as King Edward VI Almshouses, for fifteen paupers. The almshouses were rebuilt in 1782, and then again in 1829 to 1834, financed by Wyatt George Gibson, with a later block added by the Gibsons in 1840 and 1888. The 1834 buildings are the ones shown in the image above. In the 1950s, thanks to a bequest by Revd Joseph Prime, the 1782 tenements were demolished and seven two-bedroomed bungalows were added to the complex (fronting onto Park Lane). Today, the almshouses provide affordable housing for people of Saffron Walden on low incomes and are run by nine trustees and a clerk. Immediately in front of the almshouses (behind the photographer) is a Saxon cemetery where one hundred and fifty skeletons were uncovered by excavations financed by George Stacey Gibson on his land in 1876. *Inset:* Gibson date plaque. (Postcard reproduced courtesy of Jane Fairweather)

Walden Lodge, Abbey Lane, *c.* 1900s

This lodge to Audley End Park was built in 1814, and thought to be designed by the architect Thomas Rickman, who also designed Keeper's Lodge at Audley End. An extension (on the right of the modern picture) was built onto Walden Lodge in 1977. The Edwardian postcard was photographed from the Audley End park side of the gates, the modern image photographed from the Saffron Walden side in Abbey Lane.

Inside Friends' Meeting House, High Street, 1915

Saffron Walden has a long tradition of religious non-conformity, including the Society of Friends (Quakers). The first reference to Quakers in the town dates from the 1650s when two practising Quakers were punished for their faith in 1656 and 1659. By the 1670s, a room at the back of a cottage at the top of the High Street (then known as Cuckingstool End Street) was used as the first Friends' Meeting House. The Quakers continued their presence in the town and built a new Meeting House in 1791, which was enlarged in 1879. The postcard from 1915 shows that the town's branch of the British Women's Temperance Association had set up a room within the Meeting House to provide First World War soldiers with leisure facilities away from alcohol.

High Street, August 1932

The Temperance movement continued in Saffron Walden throughout the first half of the twentieth century. In August 1932 a march was held in Saffron Walden to celebrate the Centenary of Total Abstinence Pledge. The people, including a Salvation Army band, congregated just up the hill past Friends' Meeting House. Their banners included the names of John Broadbelt, Joseph Livsey, John Gratix, John King, Edward Dickinson, John Smith and David Anderton, the seven founding members of the Temperance Movement in the 1830s. The Temperance Movement spread far and wide after its foundation in the town of Preston, Lancashire; the centenary was celebrated by branches as far away as Sydney in Australia. (Postcard reproduced courtesy of Robina Veal)

High Street (Facing North), Postmarked 1904

The building on the left of the photographs is Hill House, the Victorian home of philanthropist, banker and botanist George Stacey Gibson (1813–1883) and his family. The influence of the Gibson family is still felt throughout Saffron Walden through the existence of their very many public buildings and gardens. In 1845 this branch of the Gibson family moved to Hill House in the High Street after George married Elizabeth Tuke. Gibson, a keen botanist, ensured that the house had a large well-tended and well-stocked gardens. After Gibson's only child, Mary, died in 1934, Hill House's land was sold for development. Many of the modern houses on the right side of Margaret Way (the side road in the modern photograph before Hill House) and on into the Gibson estate are on the land which was once the Gibson's extensive back garden. Hill House itself was purchased by the Post Office who had the intention of knocking it down so that a new purpose-built building could be erected. However, the Second World War stopped this from happening, and, instead, Hill House was used as a sorting office and a Telephone Exchange was built in the former gardens. Hill House has now been converted into flats.

Baptist Church, High Street, Postmarked 1908

The Baptists have worshipped in Saffron Walden since 1662, originally in the Independent Meeting House in Abbey Lane. However, in the 1770s a dispute arose between the minster and his church with the trustees of the Meeting House in Abbey Lane. The Baptists moved into a barn belonging to Elizabeth Fuller in the area of the town then known as Bailey's Lane (now Audley Road) on the junction with Cuckingstool End. With Mrs Fuller's help, they were able to build their own chapel in 1774 on the land which had housed her barn. By the 1870s, the Georgian building had served its purpose and in 1879 a new chapel was built immediately in front of the old chapel, and the old chapel was converted into a school with classrooms and a vestry. The chimney on the left side of the Edwardian image belonged to the maltings which was in nearby Gold Street.

High Street in 1833, Engraving by Charles Mottram (1807–76)

Until the mid-nineteenth century, this part of the High Street was known as Cuckingstool End Street. In the engraving above, the Walden stagecoach is travelling from London, through the Georgian streets of Saffron Walden, heading into the Market Place ready to stop at the Rose & Crown. In the early nineteenth century it was run by Matthew Winder, one of the proprietors of the Walden Coach. An important service, by the mid-eighteenth century, at least one Walden Coach ran between London and Cambridge twice weekly. However, travelling on stagecoaches could sometimes be a precarious pastime. On Wednesday 8 June 1737 stagecoaches from Saffron Walden and Bishop's Stortford, both on their way into London, were robbed at Epping. Newspapers reported that in and around the two coaches were twenty people but no one was able to capture the lone highwayman. Goods and money to the value of £6 were stolen from the Walden coach, and £4 from Stortford's coach. The culprit was none other than the infamous highwayman, Dick Turpin. According to reports, 'he used the passengers with a great deal of Civility'.

Gold Street, Early 1900s

According to Pevsner, Gold Street is 'in many ways the most delightful street in Saffron Walden' with the entire south side of St Mary The Virgin seeming 'to float above the buildings of King Street'. Pevsner is right; the street is extremely pretty, with its mix of architecture including nineteenth-century red-brick workers' houses, a large eighteenth-century house with an archway which once led through to maltings, and sixteenth-century timber-framed buildings. In modern times, the road has seen to some of the town's laundry needs with the Saffron Walden Steam Laundry Company in Gold Street since the early 1900s (but present in the town from 1897). In 1968, the Steam Laundry Company purchased the town's other laundry, the Snowflake Laundry, who operated in Castle Street. (Postcard reproduced courtesy of Jane Fairweather.) *Inset:* Pargeting of a stagecoach on a house in Gold Street.

The Baths, Hill Street (Facing Towards High Street), after 1910

The Baths in Hill Street were opened on 2 May 1910 by the mayor in front of a large crowd of spectators. The land was given to the town by Mary Wyatt Gibson, daughter of George Stacey Gibson, on the stipulation that baths would be built on her land. The baths were built by the builders Glasscock & Sons of Bishop's Stortford at a cost of £1,290. The baths had slipper baths (for people to wash in) as well as shower baths and eighteen dressing cubicles. The pool was 59 feet by 25 feet with a depth of between 3 foot (in the shallow end) and 6 foot 3 inches (in the deep end). In its early years, it was heated by exhaust steam from the town's waterworks, although this could not have created any great heat. Memories of the pool throughout its time in the town was that it was always freezing cold. In its early years the baths did not have a filtration system, so they were shut on a Sunday to allow the pool to be emptied and refilled. Because of this, admission to the baths was more expensive on a Monday (when the water was clean) than on a Saturday. The water was first chlorinated in 1939. Countless generations of children from schools all around Saffron Walden (including as far away as Cambridge and Tottenham in north London) used the baths for swimming lessons. The baths closed in 1982 and the building was demolished in 1984.

Saffron Walden Hospital, London Road, Early 1900s

Saffron Walden General Hospital was founded in 1866 and served the town for over 100 years until it closed in 1988. The hospital was financed by the generous bequest of £5,000 from Wyatt George Gibson, who died in 1862. Further money was raised by the people of the town with donations and subscriptions. The hospital was built in London Road on land owned by Lord Braybrooke of Audley End at the cost of £5,504 for the construction, £600 for furnishings, and £100 for the dispensary. The hospital employed a district nurse, who in the 1870s was paid £25 per annum and boarded at the hospital. At various stages in its 120-year history, more facilities and buildings were added; in 1935 the film star Gracie Fields opened a new children's wing which cost £3,500. After the hospital's closure, in 1990 it was converted into an office building and is now the Uttlesford District Council's Offices.

London Road (Facing Towards Audley Road), Early 1900s

Standing in the doorway of his shop is David Miller (1868–1936) who owned a bakery and confectionary shop on London Road. Miller, a very well-respected figure in Saffron Walden, became the mayor six times between 1920 and 1930 and also served on the Town Council for twenty-five years. On his first election as mayor in 1920, he gave three guineas to the first male child born in Saffron Walden during his tenure as mayor, and his wife gave the same to the first female child. He died in 1936 aged sixty-eight in Hastings where he had retired. The bakery and confectionary shop passed on to David's son Edgar M. Miller and finally to his grandson, another David Miller, who also became mayor of Saffron Walden in the 1970s. (Postcard reproduced courtesy of Jean Harrison)

Ladies' Training College, South Road, Postmarked 1935

Saffron Walden Ladies' Training College was built in the 1880s from George Stacey Gibson's money (who died during the building's construction) and was officially opened in May 1884. In 1885, two years after pupils first arrived at the college, twenty-seven women, who had been through an intensive two-year training course, left the college to become elementary school teachers. This was the first cohort of the many hundreds of young trainee-teachers who passed through the college's doors, including men in its later years. Nearly a hundred years later, in 1977, the college ceased as a teacher-training college. The college then became Bell College, a private international school owned by the British Foreign Schools Society for up to 250 pupils. In 2007, the international college shut its doors, and in the 2010s the building became a new housing development, Bell College Court.

Friends' School, Mount Pleasant Road, *c.* 1900s

In 1875, after an outbreak of typhoid, the Friends' School, a boarding school for the education of both boys and girls, which had been founded in Clerkenwell in 1702, moved from Croydon to Saffron Walden. A new school for fifty-eight boys and thirty-two girls was constructed in 1877–1879 in Mount Pleasant Road on land owned by Saffron Walden's premier Quaker family, the Gibsons. Today the school still flourishes as a day and boarding school, for boys and girls from nursery age to sixth form.

Debden Road and Water Tower, after May 1913
The Water Tower on Debden Road was built in 1913 by Saffron Walden Town Council, with its foundation stone laid by the mayor, Dr J. P. Atkinson senior. The tower was built to a depth of eight feet in the ground, and ninety feet above ground, at an estimated cost of £2,270. Approximately 32,000 bricks and 140 tons of concrete were used in its construction. The town stopped using the water tower in the 1960s, after which time nearby Friends' School incorporated the tower into their grounds. (Postcard reproduced courtesy of Jane Fairweather.)

The Common, Postmarked 1904

Saffron Walden's picturesque Common is one of the town's treasures. It is a local beauty spot which today attracts dog-walkers, joggers, tobogganing children, and picnicking families. It has also been used for the celebrations of high days and holidays, including celebrations of national events such as royal coronations, jubilees and marriages. At the coronation of George IV in 1821, an ox was roasted on the Common and the townsfolk were also given twelve barrels of stout. The day was one of great celebrations; however, local newspaper reports totally conflict in their accounts of the day. The *Cambridge Chronicle and Journal* recounted how the day began with the ringing of bells and hoisting of flags on the church and castle. The ox was roasted on the common and its meat distributed in an orderly fashion. This report of an orderly ox-roast is in total contrast to the *Bury and Norwich Post*, who told how there were nearly riots on the Common when the crowd heard that George IV's queen, Caroline of Brunswick, had not been allowed to attend his coronation. The town heard about poor Caroline's fate as they were roasting the ox and because Caroline was a popular figure, the news so incensed people that it 'operated on the feelings of a large party like an electric shock. In a moment the carcass of the bullock was attacked, literally torn by piecemeal off the spit, and scattered in every direction; the expected meal being sacrificed to their indignation'.

Inset: Water fountain on the common, with the inscription. 'This fountain was erected and 169 additional trees were planted along the south side and in other parts of this recreation ground to commemorate the jubilee of the reign of her most gracious majesty Queen Victoria AD 1887'.

Saffron Walden Grammar School, Ashdon Road, Early 1900s

The town's former grammar school was founded in 1522 by Dame Joan Bradbury (c.1450–1530) who re-established an existing school. Dame Bradbury was the wife of the Lord Mayor of London, and sister of John Leche (died 1521), vicar of St Mary's. Her original sixteenth-century school was next to St Mary's churchyard, and it became King Edward VI grammar school in 1549. In 1655 a new school was built in Castle Street, where it remained for over two hundred years. In 1881, the school moved to new premises in Ashdon Road, financed by Lord Braybrooke and George Stacey Gibson. The grammar school ceased during the Second World War when it became the control centre for the United States Army Air Force's 65th fighter wing. Directly after the war, part of the building became a junior school known as Dame Bradbury's School, whilst the other part became a hostel for students at the Teacher Training College. Today, the school is still known as Dame Bradbury's and is an independent school for children up to eleven years of age, under the Stephen Perse Foundation. *Inset:* One of the grammar school's most famous pupils was Revd (Edward) Noel Mellish (1880–1962), an army chaplain during the First World War who was awarded the Victoria Cross in 1916 for rescuing twenty-two severely wounded men at St Elio, Belgium. After the war, Mellish returned to Essex and was the vicar of St Mary's Great Dunmow from 1928 to 1948.

Camille Cecile Holland, Saffron Walden Cemetery, Postmarked 1906

In March 1903, newspapers all over Britain were full of details about Samuel Herbert Dougal, who had been arrested for forging the signature of a Miss Holland. During the subsequent investigation, it became known that Camille Cecile Holland, a wealthy spinster, had not been seen for four years. Dougal had told people that she had gone abroad. But as she was a woman in her late fifties who had not previously had desires to travel, this seemed unlikely, particularly as she had been in regular correspondence with her family until at least mid-1899. Attention switched to her farmhouse, the Moat Farm, in nearby Clavering and on 20 March, the police started to search for her body. On Easter Monday (13 April), crowds of approximately six thousand people swarmed to her farm to watch the police dig. On Monday 27 April, the police found her remains at her farm in a filled-in ditch, with a bullet lodged in her head. Miss Holland was buried in Saffron Walden's cemetery on 12 May 1903. Dougal was hanged for her murder on 14 July 1903 at Springfield County Gaol near Chelmsford. *Inset:* Samuel Dougal escorted from Audley End station by two policemen, 1903. (Postcard reproduced courtesy of Jean Harrison)

Thaxted Road, Early 1900s

In the Edwardian photograph is the bridge which carried the now defunct railway branch line which ran from Audley End to Bartlow. The bridge has since been demolished and only its supports on both sides of the road still exist. Next to the bridge is The Gate public house. The house on the left appears to be a fine Georgian house, but the date on its front is 1849 and thus the house's appearance is not in keeping with this date. Census returns show that this was once the house of William Green who was a 'bricklayer' in the 1841 census; but by 1851 described as 'master bricklayer employing 4 men and 2 boys'. It would seem that William Green, master builder of Saffron Walden, had celebrated his new status by renovating his house, then in a quiet country lane, and included his importance within its brickwork. The emblem on the date-plaque depicts a builder's 'setting-out tool' at the top, and a brick cutting tool (or brick axe) at the bottom. William was the father of Elijah and Julius, both well-known local builders. Julius Green also ran the Duke of York pub at the top of the High Street and caused much local gossip in 1870 when he married the landlady, who was his deceased wife's step-mother. The Greens were active builders and lime-burners in the town until at least the early 1910s. It is possibly members of the Green family who were standing outside their house in the Edwardian photograph. *Inset:* William Green's date plaque celebrating his new status as a master bricklayer.

CHAPTER 2

Audley End

Audley End House, Engraving Produced in 1808 Showing the House *c.* **1676**

The grand Jacobean house at Audley End was built between *c.* 1605 and 1614 by Thomas Howard, the 1st Earl of Suffolk and Baron Howard de Walden, at the cost of £200,000, on the site of the former Walden Abbey. In 1538, Henry VIII seized Walden Abbey and gave it to his Lord Chancellor, Sir Thomas Audley (*c.* 1488–1544), who converted the abbey into his own extensive residence. When Sir Thomas Audley died, his house passed down to his descendants through his daughter's line to the Howards. The house stayed in the ownership of the Earls of Suffolk until they could no longer afford the magnificent house, and the 3rd Earl sold it to Charles II in 1668, who used it on his way to and from the races at Newmarket. At the end of the seventeenth century, Sir Christopher Wren was employed to carry out extensive renovations to the house. However, the cost of maintaining the house with its estate was prohibitive to the crown. In 1701, the House was returned to the Howard family by William III. After this time, substantial alterations were made to make the House smaller, including demolishing part of the outer court (seen in the drawing above) and remodelling some of the interior. In 1724, Daniel Defoe, in his *Tour Through The Eastern Counties,* commented that the House was in ruins and was decaying.

Audley End in 1810, Including St Mary's, Saffron Walden in the Distance

The house and estate stayed in the Howard family until their line died out in 1745 and the estate was divided by four co-heirs. One of whom was Elizabeth, Countess of Portsmouth, who purchased the house and part of the parklands from the other co-heirs in 1751. The Countess agreed to leave her estate to her nephew, Sir John Whitwell, provided he legally changed his surname to Griffin, which he did in 1749. After her death in 1762, Sir John Griffin Griffin inherited Audley End House and some of the parklands. In 1788 Sir John became the 1st Lord Braybrooke; thus started a long succession of Lords Braybrooke of Audley End. The Lords Braybrooke stayed at Audley End House until the house was requisitioned by the government during the Second World War and used as a training school for undercover Polish agents. In 1948, the 9th Lord Braybrooke sold Audley End House to the nation for £30,000, in lieu of death duties, with its furniture and paintings given on permanent loan. In 1984, English Heritage took over responsibility for the house. In modern times, it has become one of the most popular tourist attractions in East Anglia with over 143,000 visitors in 2013.

Inset: Lion Entrance to Audley End house, built in 1786.

Audley End House and the River Cam, c. 1900s

Richard Griffin Neville (1783–1858) inherited Audley End House in 1825 and was the 3rd Lord Braybrooke. He was resident in Audley End House during census night of 30 March 1851 and from this return, a sense of the house's Victorian size and every-day operations upstairs and downstairs can be gleaned. Lord Braybrooke's occupation was described as 'English Peer, 1340 acres, 100 men, 31 carpenters'. Also present at the house were various members of his family including his wife, two daughters and two sons. The census reveals that a tremendous number of servants were employed to look after the Braybrookes. The house contained a retired governess, a surgeon, a housekeeper, four ladies maids, four laundry maids, five house maids, two still-room maids, one dairy maid, two kitchen maids, one scullery maid, a butler, a groom of the chamber, an under-butler, four footmen, a baker, a house boy, and a general servant to Lord Braybrooke's eldest son. The only absence is that of the cook; she, perhaps, was away the night of the census. This was, of course, only those who lived and served inside the house. The census returns for the buildings and houses around the main house reveal farm bailiffs, gamekeepers, farm labourers, lodge keepers, woodmen, agricultural labours and shepherds.

The Abbey, Audley End, Postmarked 1906

In the village of Audley End is the building now known as St Mark's College. It was built as almshouses between 1604 and 1614 by Thomas Howard, 1st Earl of Suffolk (1561–1626), to house twenty elderly people. Their accommodation was contained around two courts, with a chapel, hall and kitchen and built on the site of Walden Abbey's infirmary. The infirmary had been used by the Benedictine Abbey of Walden from the thirteenth century until the reign of Henry VIII. Unusually for a religious house, Henry VIII did not dissolve Walden Abbey by the Suppression of Religious Houses Acts of 1536 and 1539, but rather the abbey ceased to be after the last abbot resigned (either voluntary or was forced) in the late 1530s during a scandal when it was revealed to Thomas Cromwell that the abbot had married. The abbey was granted to William More, the suffragan Bishop of Colchester. The king seized the abbey from Bishop More on the 22 March 1538, and sold it to Sir Thomas Audley on 27 March 1538.

The Abbey, Audley End, *c.* 1910s

Thomas Howard's almshouses were disbanded in 1633. During the eighteenth and nineteenth century, the abbey building was used as a farm by Audley End House. In the late 1940s, the abbey buildings were given by Lord Braybrook to the Diocese of Chelmsford for its conversion into a retirement home for clergymen. On 28 September 1951, the building was dedicated by the Bishop of Chelmsford as St Mark's College, a retirement home for ten elderly clergy and their wives, along with two single clergymen. The architect for the conversion was Marshall Sisson, the surveyor to the Royal Academy. The old kitchen became the college's dining hall, the chapel was restored and rebuilt, and the old hall became the new college's common room. In the 1990s, St Mark's College changed its purpose and became an activity and education centre for young people within the diocese of Chelmsford. *Inset:* 1818 engraving by J. Grieg of the almshouses when they were used as farm buildings.

Audley End Village, *c.* 1900s

This tiny road leading down to St Mark's College is all that is left of the once very busy and active medieval village of Brook Walden, which had its own weekly market and annual August fair. In 1579, a contemporary pamphlet, written about the notorious witchcraft trials at Chelmsford's assizes described how Mother Staunton of Wimbish had been accused of bewitching various people within Brook Walden. She was not tried for murder, but the pamphleteer took great pains to describe her alleged witchcraft activities. This included her causing the cradle of a child of Brook Walden to rock itself furiously in the presence of the Earl of Surrey's gentleman. In the late eighteenth century, the 1st Lord Braybrooke demolished many houses in Brook Walden, including houses on what was once Audley End's High Street but is now the main Audley End Road from Saffron Walden. The majority of the houses seen in these images were built during the late eighteenth century and are of timber-frame with plaster construction. The road also still contains a sixteenth century hall and a medieval hall house. On the left side of the images is a building which was once the village's school, and later became the post office (closed in 2009). On the right is a row of tiny houses, built by Lord Braybrooke and used as almshouses throughout the nineteenth century for eight elderly pauper women.

CHAPTER 3

Littlebury Parish

Littlebury Green, 2015

The modern-day civil parish of Littlebury comprises of the village of Littlebury, along with the three hamlets of Littlebury Green, Catmere End, and Chapel Green. At the time of the William the Conqueror's Domesday survey of 1086, the manor of Littlebury was in the possession of Ely Abbey and had a population of twenty-eight households. After the Dissolution of the Monasteries by Henry VIII, the crown retained the manor of Littlebury and it was leased by Thomas Sutton from the 1560s. In the early 1600s, Sutton purchased the manor, which his estate then sold to Thomas Howard, 1st Earl of Suffolk. The Earls of Suffolk continued to remain the owners of the manor of Littlebury until the last Earl died intestate in 1745. In the 1760s, Littlebury manor became the property of Sir John Griffin Griffin, who became the 1st Lord Braybrooke in 1788. Part of Audley End House is within the parish of Littlebury, including the House's sixteenth century stables, and some of the House's extensive parklands.

In 1841, the population of the village of Littlebury was 822 people with 169 houses. In 1851, the hamlets of Chapel Green had four houses, Littlebury Green had thirty-two houses (two of which were 'beer-houses'), and Catmere End had twenty-eight houses. In 2008, the parish's population was 240 houses in Littlebury village, fifty-three houses in Littlebury Green, twenty-five houses in Catmere End, and one house in Chapel Green. There are two churches in the parish of Littlebury: Holy Trinity in Littlebury village and St Peters, a chapel-of-ease, in Littlebury Green (built 1885). Chapel Green once had its own chapel (hence its name) but nothing now remains of this building.

Inset: St Peter's Littlebury Green chapel.

Littlebury Village Centre, Early 1900s

This Edwardian street scene of the main crossroads in the village, where the Cambridge Road meets the Walden Road and Littlebury's High Street, was photographed sometime in the early 1900s. By the 1910s, the crossroad's signpost had moved from the wall outside the post office to the centre of the road. The modern-day photograph shows that the village's planners have at some point thought it prudent to remove the signpost from the middle of the road and so it is now tucked away next to the village sign. The house on the right (blue in the modern photograph) was the village's post office and dates from the seventeenth and eighteenth centuries. *Inset:* Littlebury's village sign and crossroad's signpost.

High Street, Littlebury, Early 1900s

On the left side of both images is High House, a three-storey building built in the late eighteenth century during the Georgian era of fine house-building. Its front, a mock Tudor façade, was added during the nineteenth century. The children on the right are standing by the front entrance gateway leading through to the church's Rectory. The tall chimney in the centre-right of the Edwardian image is that of the Queen's Head, built in the fifteenth century. In the eighteenth and early nineteenth centuries, the inn was used by stage and mail coaches on their way to London in the south, or to Newmarket or Norwich in the north. Just before the pub is a small single-storey red-brick building, The Reading Room, which dates from 1852. This was built by Joseph Wix, who was the vicar of Holy Trinity church between 1840 and 1889. *Inset:* The Reading Room, now converted into a garage belonging to The Old Coach House.

The Village of Littlebury

Walden Road, Littlebury, c. 1930s

Walden Road in the nineteenth and twentieth centuries included some of the village's shops and pubs, but the buildings are now converted to residential houses. The range of buildings on the right included the village's bakery and a general store. Further down the road is The Old Carpenter's Arms, which, according to trade directories, was run by various members of the Abraham family from the 1860s until the 1930s. The Abrahams of the Carpenter's Arms also had other trades, including carpenters, wheelwrights, undertakers and builders. The building on the left has had its thatch removed and bedrooms inserted into the roof area.

Littlebury Mill and Mill House, Postmarked 1905

William the Conqueror's 1086 tax survey of his land, Domesday, recorded that the manor of Littlebury had five mills. It is highly likely, therefore, that the present mill, known as King's Mill and built in the eighteenth century, was built on the site of one of those original pre-Norman mills. In 1815, the miller was Thomas King who married Mary Portway of New (Little) Sampford in June 1815. By the time of the 1861 census, the miller was Walter M. King who also farmed fifty acres and employed two labourers and two boys. Ten years later Walter had died, but his son, Thomas, was the miller. In 1871, this Thomas King employed eight men and four boys at his mill, along with fourteen men and five boys on his 220 acre farm. In 1881, Thomas King had become so successful that he lived in Granta House, a large house next to the church. The mill continued to function as a flour mill up until the twentieth century, but is now a residential house. Attached to the mill is the Mill House, built at the same time as the mill. During the Second World War, Audley End House was requisitioned by the government and the Dowager Lady Braybrooke moved to the Mill House in 1943, where she lived until her death in the 1970s. *Inset:* Granta House.

Holy Trinity Church, Littlebury, *c.* 1920s

The original flint and stone church was built in the Anglo-Norman period and had alterations made to it from the twelfth to fifteenth centuries. In the 1870s, the architect Edward Barr of Saffron Walden substantially renovated the church chiefly funded by the 5th Lord Braybrooke, but also by subscriptions and offertories raised from the villagers. Barr restored the nave and aisles, replaced all the windows (except those in the tower) and removed all the old pews. He also added a chancel, vestry and organ chamber at a cost of approximately £2,000. The Braybrooke family continued their association with Littlebury in death with three generations of Lords and Ladies Braybrooke buried in the churchyard. *Inset:* (Top) The south porch was built in the early sixteenth century, following bequest made in two wills dating from 1504 and 1505. (Bottom) The five marble headstones and graves containing the Lords Braybrooke of Audley End, with nearly all of their Ladies Braybrooke.

Littlebury War Memorial, Holy Trinity
Churchyard, 1920s

Seventy-nine men and women of Littlebury
village served during the First World War;
of those, twenty-four died, including two
who died of illnesses whilst on active
service. These two are buried in Holy
Trinity's churchyard: Brigadier General
Colin Lawrence MacNab (died aged
forty-seven on 13 October 1918) and Sister
Ada Ann Woodley (died aged thirty-two
on 10 January 1918) of the Second Western
Hospital (Manchester), Territorial Force
Nursing Service. Sister Woodley was the
daughter of Mrs S. Perrin of Littlebury.
She left the village sometime before 1911 to
become a hospital nurse in Rochdale. She
was posthumously awarded the Silver War
Badge on the 27 January 1918, her gravestone
has the inscription 'She hath done what she
could'. *Inset:* Sister Ada Ann Woodley's grave
in Littlebury churchyard.

The Rectory, Littlebury, *c.* 1920s

This is the back of the vicarage, and shows the house's extension which was built by Joseph Wix in the nineteenth century, during his tenure as the vicar of Holy Trinity church. The 'rectory' was a vicarage for use by the vicar and so was not inhabited by the village's rector (a non-residential sinecure post). The house was originally built in the sixteenth century, and has now been split into two large semi-detached houses known as North House and South House. Joseph Wix's vicarage was a large establishment; the house had its own coach house and stabling built during Wix's time at Holy Trinity. This too has been converted into a private house and is now known as The Old Coach House. *Inset:* Joseph Wix's Coach House.

Howe Close, Catmere End, *c.* 1920s

This row of houses in the hamlet of Catmere End within the parish of Littlebury was built by the local council in the 1920s or 1930s. The postcard shows the doorways of at least fourteen houses; however, today's photograph demonstrates that only four of those fourteen houses still exist, and those that remain have been substantially altered.

CHAPTER 4

Wendens Ambo

St Mary the Virgin Church, *c.* 1900s
Wendens Ambo was once two tiny
Essex villages: Great Wenden (or
Wenden Magna) and Little Wenden (or
Wenden Parva). The Latin word *ambo*
means 'both', and thus is the meaning
of Wendens Ambo's name, 'both
Wendens'. Both villages were listed in
the Domesday Book and were joined
together to form the united Wendens
Ambo in 1662. Until that date, both
villages had their own churches, but
Little Wenden's church ceased to be
used and was probably derelict by the
time of the villages' union. There is
no longer any trace of Little Wenden's
church. Great Wenden's parish
church, St Mary the Virgin, became
the church of the united Wendens
Ambo. According to an 1848 trade
directory of Essex, Wendens Ambo
had 347 inhabitants. This figure has
changed little in the last 150 years; it
is estimated that today's population
stands at just over 360 inhabitants.

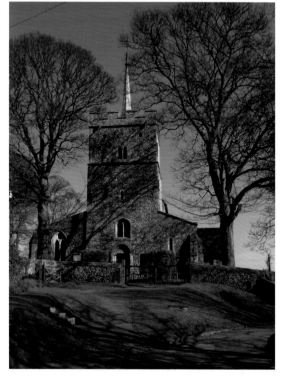

Bell Inn, c. 1920s

The Bell Inn was built in the late sixteenth century and first appeared in documents dating from the 1570s. It has served the village for nearly 450 years. The census of 1861 documents that at this stage in its history, the landlord was George Savill, who was also the enumerator for the village's census return. In 1871, George was still listed as the being at The Old Bell, but was described as being a farmer of 70 acres, employing two men, and a boy.

The Post Office, c. 1900s

Before the arrival of the trains in the 1840s, the village of Wendens Ambo was a rural community with its inhabitants working in agricultural occupations. Local newspapers from the nineteenth century show that little crime was reported in the village, and when it was reported, it was mainly connected with rural crime. If local newspapers had been in existence at the beginning of the seventeenth century, they would have been full of the crimes of a local sheep rustler, William Newton, a shepherd of Great Wenden. In 1601 Newton appeared at the Brentwood assizes, charged with grand larceny. In the summer of 1600, he and Stephen Marshall of Wimbish stole twenty-two sheep (to the value of £10) from Arkesden and thirty sheep (£10) from Littlebury. In the winter of 1600, the pair (with another accomplice) stole a further twenty-six sheep (£5) from Newport. William Newton, shepherd of Great Wenden, was found guilty but allowed to plead the benefit of clergy. Benefit of clergy was a medieval loop-hole in the law which carried on into the nineteenth century, with various reforms over the centuries. At the time of Newton's trial, claiming benefit of clergy meant that he was a first-time offender and was able to read a passage from the Bible. Pleading such, he was likely to have been branded on thumb and his case transferred to the ecclesiastical (church) courts for sentencing. The ecclesiastical courts always had lighter sentences for first offenders. Great Wenden's sheep rustler probably escaped hanging, and, instead, received a prison sentence of a few years.

Wenden Hill Cottage, *c.* 1900s

Wendens Ambo has a large number of picturesque cottages. According to Uttlesford District Council's 2013 Conservation Report, 25 per cent of Wendens Ambo's listed buildings have thatched roofs. Although beautiful, a few of Wendens Ambo's cottages have, in the past, been scenes of devastating fires. In April 1881, the local newspapers reported how four large families, consisting of thirty-two people, were made homeless after a chimney in one of their cottages caught fire and flames ripped through the rest of the buildings. The four families lost everything in the blaze. The small tight-knit community of Wendens Ambo rallied round the homeless families with neighbours taking in some families and others finding temporary homes in nearby villages.

Church Path, c. 1900s

Church Path is one of the prettiest approaches to any English village church. The view shown in these images has adorned many lids to fancy chocolate-boxes during the 1970s and 1980s, and is also often used today in modern wall calendars of English villages. The buildings in Church Path date from between the sixteenth and eighteenth centuries, and some have had minor modern alterations. No. 2 Church Path (the middle two buildings in the postcard) was probably a late medieval/early Tudor guildhall. Whether this guildhall was for trade or religious purposes is unknown. With its proximity to the church, perhaps it was a religious guildhall. In the 1870s, there was a tiny infants' school in Church Path, run by one of the house's residents in her home. Until 1881, this was the village's only school.

Duck Street, *c.* 1920s/1930s

This pretty spot is the ford in Duck Street over a tributary of the River Cam. Duck Street dates from medieval times, although it was possibly used much earlier. In 2006, Essex County Council's Field Archaeology Unit carried out an investigation in a field to the west of the junction between Duck Street and Rookery Lane. They discovered evidence of Roman topography from the first century AD and also pottery from the second and third centuries. There was also evidence of medieval activity within the area from the twelfth to the sixteenth century. Today, the road is very near to both the railway line at nearby Audley End Station, and the M11 motorway.

Samuel Herbert Dougal Arriving at Audley End Station, Spring 1903

In 1845, the station at Wendens Ambo was built on the land of the Audley End estate. Originally named Wendens after the village, the station was renamed a few years later to Audley End station and its name has remained thus to this day. Guests of Lord Braybrooke arrived by train at the station and then were taken by carriage to his house. The station's fine entrance porch was built to provide shade and shelter for Lord Braybrooke's visitors whilst they awaited their grand carriages. Today, the station is used by commuters predominantly working in London or Cambridge, and so brings a daily onslaught of cars into the station's car park from neighbouring towns and villages. The station currently has 664 car parking spaces, compared to 374 spaces at Cambridge (up-line) and 477 spaces at Bishop's Stortford (down-line). The sheer number of parking spaces alone shows the extent to which Wendens Ambo is used merely as a stopping point for busy commuters on their daily hurry to and from work. It is curious that there are nearly two spaces in the station's car park for every single person who lives in Wendens Ambo.

Railway Cottages, Postmarked 1907

The pretty row of flint and red brick cottages was built in the 1840s by the 3rd Lord Braybrooke to accommodate workers on the new railway. The row of cottages comprises of nine dwelling places. In the census of 1851, two of the houses were uninhabited, the rest of the houses were occupied by railway labourers and porters in their twenties and thirties, together with their families. In the 1861 census, the terrace was then known as New Row but by the time of the 1871 census, known as Railway Cottages. The postcard was sent by Lily in 1907, she wrote on the back, 'I thought you would like this PC. One of them with the bike is me. I expect you will know which one. It was taken when I was going to Walden the other week. I had got a lot of parcels on behind'.

Neville Arms, Station Road, *c.* 1900s

In January 1845, newspapers reported that the 3rd Lord Braybrooke was building a new hotel at Wendens Ambo station. The hotel was named the Neville Arms after Lord Braybrooke's family surname. Between 1845 and 1894, the Saich family were the hotel's licensed victuallers. George John Saich was the landlord until the early 1870s, after which time his son Walter took over the hotel. On the 5 July 1894, Walter (then in his early forties) died unexpectedly from blood poisoning and his wife, Elizabeth, died at 9.30 p.m. the very same evening of pleurisy. They left behind ten orphaned children. This was the end of Saich family's fifty years at the hotel. Today the Neville Arms is used as suites of offices and a dental practice.

CHAPTER 5

The Chesterfords

South Street and Carmel Street Junction, Great Chesterford, Early 1900s
The settlement of Great Chesterford, on the Essex/Cambridgeshire border, has been occupied throughout time by differing peoples who have all left their trace within its landscape. This includes tribes from the late Iron Age period and, later, the Romano-British who built a fort in AD 60, and a wall enclosing the Roman town in the fourth century. By the time of Domesday (1086), the village consisted of fifty-three households, and had good resources such as one thousand pigs in its woodland and three mills. In the early 1870s, the village consisted of 215 houses with a population of just over 1,000 people. In 2001, the population was 1,450. Today, the pretty village is abundantly served with its fast road and rail connections. However, progress comes at a price: many of the modern images in this chapter were photographed early on a Sunday morning. Even then, the roar of the nearby motorway traffic was very evident throughout the rural picturesque villages of Great and Little Chesterford. *Inset:* Great Chesterford's village sign.

Mill Stream, Great Chesterford, Postmarked 1911

The Mill Stream runs alongside Great Chesterford's water corn mill (out of shot in the Edwardian image, but to the photographer's right). The mill at Great Chesterford was documented by William the Conqueror in 1086, who recorded that the settlement had three mills. However, there has probably been at least one mill in the village stretching back to its Roman occupation. In the late seventeenth century until the mid-nineteenth century, Great Chesterford's mill was run by the Sampson family. In 1857, the Sampsons left Great Chesterford to become tobacco manufacturers in Woolwich, and put their mill up for sale. The advertisement for the sale specified that the mill was being sold along with a new family residence, outbuildings and pleasure grounds. By the end of the nineteenth century and on into the twentieth century, the mill was owned by the King family, from whom the mill takes its current name, King's Mill. The steam mill seen today was built in the late nineteenth century, and is now residential flats.

Crown Inn and Posting House, Great Chesterford, Postmarked 1913

The current inn was built in the late eighteenth century, replacing an earlier inn which had been present at the same location since at least the early seventeenth century. The inn was on the London to Newmarket stagecoach route and the trade brought its owners much prosperity. In October 1671, the diarist and writer John Evelyn (1620–1706) travelled from London on a stagecoach to meet the king, who was at Newmarket. The journey took Evelyn only a few hours as the stagecoach changed its six horses three times, the last time at Great Chesterford (presumably at the Crown Inn). By 1841, the inn was also a successful posting house for mail, and had at least forty-three pairs of horses available for hire, along with four daily stagecoaches. The inn's fortunes must have declined severely when the great train age arrived in the village in 1848. Today Crown House is still a hotel, with eighteen bedrooms and a restaurant; although, alas, it no longer has any stagecoaches at its disposal.

Manor Lane, Great Chesterford, Early 1900s

In the past, rural villages, such as Great Chesterford, were tight-knit communities. In an age before modern communication, transport and medicine, often women who were not living in the norms of society were accused of acts of witchcraft against their neighbours. In Elizabethan Great Chesterford, there were two women accused by their neighbours of being witches, mother and daughter, Elizabeth and Jane Morrisbee. Elizabeth had first come to the attention of the Archdeaconry Court in 1579 and Jane a year later in 1580, both accused of witchcraft. In 1584, Elizabeth appeared at the Witham Assizes when she was accused of bewitching her neighbour Agnes Wynterflodd and causing her death in December 1582. She was also accused of bewitching Jane, the daughter of Thomas Rowlande, another neighbour. Elizabeth was found guilty and hanged.

Reflections at Great Chesterford, *c.* 1920s

The River Cam appears to maunder serenely through the village of Great Chesterford. However, the tranquillity of these scenes has not always been the case. In May 1824, heavy rains had produced high flood waters throughout England and nearly caused a tragedy in Great Chesterford. The London to Norwich stagecoach, *The Magnet,* had just crossed the river on the Great Chesterford Bridge, when part of the bridge collapsed with a tremendous crash. Water poured onto the road for half a mile, with the depth as high as the horses' bellies. The guard on *The Magnet* was able to get his coach to the Crown House Inn and warn an oncoming mail-coach by flashing a lantern. The mail coach was only just able to stop in time; its guard unloaded his passengers onto a small section of the bridge which was still standing, turned the mail coach around, recovered his passengers and retreated back along the road. Just moments later, the remains of the bridge, including where the passengers had just been precariously waiting, was washed away by the torrents of water which reached 15 feet.

The Vicarage, Great Chesterford, Postmarked 1908

Great Chesterford's Vicarage was built in the late fifteenth century, with its plaster detail added in the seventeenth century. There is alleged to be a secret underground passageway which ran between the church, the vicarage and Crown House Inn. In the 1920s, the Vicarage was used by the Revd Robert Doble as a cramming school for boys wishing to pass Cambridge University's entrance exams. In recent years, the vicarage has been renamed Bishops House in honour of incumbents who went on to become bishops, including Charles Blomfield (1786–1857) who became the Bishop of Chester in the 1820s. *Inset:* Back of the Vicarage, postmarked 1928.

The Village Lt Chesterford.

144880

High Street, Little Chesterford, Postmarked 1938

Domesday of 1086 recorded that the village of Little Chesterford, in the Hundred of Uttlesford, had twenty-seven households, a fairly large village for the time. Eight hundred years later in the nineteenth century, the size of village had not kept up with the passage of time, having only just doubled in size. In 1861, the census records that there were fifty-five inhabited houses, with a total of 278 people at home that night. Amongst the village's inhabitants were two grocers, a shoemaker, a maltster, a rat-catcher, two licensed victuallers/beerhouse keepers, a gentleman's gardener, a game-keeper, two farmers of large farms, a butcher, a washerwoman, three paupers, a Chelsea pensioner and numerous agricultural labourers. The census return for 2011 notes that the population of the village was 215.

St Mary the Virgin, Little Chesterford, Postmarked 1913

Little Chesterford's church was built in the thirteenth century with the east windows added in the late fourteenth century. The church was renovated by the architect James Barr in the 1855 to include a vestry and bell-cot for the church's two bells. The church is annexed to the vicarage of Great Chesterford, with the vicar of Great Chesterford also holding the position as the rector of Little Chesterford. In the distance of the modern photograph is The Manor, an early thirteenth-century manor house which was partially rebuilt and changed from the fourteenth to sixteenth centuries. Grade I listed, it is one of the oldest inhabited manor houses in Essex. *Inset:* The former Victorian school, now the village hall (built 1862).

The Street, Lt. Chesterford.   78712

The Crown, High Street, Little Chesterford, *c.* 1920s/1930s

On 7 April 1914, the tiny village of Little Chesterford was nearly destroyed when a devastating fire, thought to have started by a spark from a passing steam traction engine, swept through the village destroying nearly everything in its path. The fire started in an outbuilding of Bordeaux Farm, but winds carried burning material from the original seat of the fire so it spread throughout the entire village. Eyewitness accounts record how men ran in from the nearby fields in an attempt to put the flames out, whilst women gathered their children and escaped from their burning homes. Between nine and eleven houses were totally destroyed, along with two farms and two pubs (including The Crown shown on this page). Over forty people were made homeless, with most not being able to save any of their possessions. A great deal of the village's livestock was burnt alive. Newspaper reports told how fire pumps from nearby Saffron Walden, Great Chesterford, Hinxton, Audley End and Chesterford Park had to attend the blaze as the village's own pump was inadequate. It is incredible that no one lost their life.

High Street, Little Chesterford, *c.* 1920s/1930s

One of the victims of the 1914 fire was Rebecca Law, then aged 101. At the time of the fire, she lived in Little Chesterford with her son and her granddaughter's family. Bedridden, she was carried out of their burning house in her night-dress in a wheel-barrow. Just months before the fire, four generations of her family had appeared in many newspapers around the Britain advertising the family's use of the medical ointment Zam-Buk. After a long life, Rebecca died shortly before her 103rd birthday, still with all her faculties, in Saffron Walden Workhouse, where she had been sent after the fire made her homeless. Prior to moving in with her family, she had lived for over thirty years in one of the tiny white almshouses in Audley End village. Her obituary stated

> Sixty years ago she was left a widow with seven children, only one of whom was at work, earning 1s 6d a week. She supported the family working the fields in the summer, and sack-making and washing in the winter. She had thirty-five grandchildren and forty-six great grandchildren. Asked recently what she attributed her long life, she said: 'Hard work and plenty of it. No woman has worked harder than I have and I was never happier than when at work. I love everybody. If I did not, I should not have lived so long.'

It is fitting that this book ends with the story of one of Uttlesford's most resilient of characters, who lived her long life in the towns and villages of this book. Rebecca Law, born 1813 in Wendens Ambo, lived in Littlebury Green, Audley End and Little Chesterford, died January 1916 in Saffron Walden. *Inset:* Mrs Law in hospital after the fire.

Bibliography

While writing *Saffron Walden & Around Through Time*, the following books, reports and websites proved absolutely invaluable. This is by no means a complete bibliography, but simply the resources I consulted. To those historians, commentators and surveyors who went before me, I owe a debt of gratitude.

Books

Anon, *A Detection of damnable driftes, practized by three VVitches arraigned at Chelmisforde in Essex, at the laste Assises there holden, whiche were executed in Aprill* (London, 1579).

Anon, 'Littlebury', in *An Inventory of the Historical Monuments in Essex, Volume 1* (London: His Majesty's Stationery Office, 1916).

Anon, 'Saffron Walden', in *An Inventory of the Historical Monuments in Essex, Volume 1* (London: His Majesty's Stationery Office, 1916).

Cockburn, J.S., *Calendar of Assize Records: Essex Indictments – Elizabeth I* (London: Her Majesty's Stationery Office, 1978).

Cockburn, J.S., *Calendar of Assize Records: Essex Indictments – James I* (London: Her Majesty's Stationery Office, 1982).

Coward, B., *Oliver Cromwell: Profiles in Power* (Routledge, 2000).

Defoe, D., *Tour Through the Eastern Counties* (Ipswich: East Anglian Magazine Limited; 1949)

Essex County Council Field Archaeology Unit, *Duck Street, Wendens Ambo* (Essex: Essex County Council, 2006).

Essex County Council, *Saffron Walden Town Trail* (Essex: Essex County Council, 2014).

Neville, R. (Lord Braybrooke), *The History of Audley End*, (London, 1836).

Page, W., and Horace J., (eds.) 'Houses of Benedictine monks: Abbey of Walden', in *A History of the County of Essex: Volume 2* (London: Victoria County History, 1907).

Pevsner, N. and Bettley, J. *The buildings of England: Essex* (London: Yale University Press, 2010).

Pike, R., *The Victor Heroes* (Saffron Walden: Ancre Publishers, 2000).

Player, J., *Sketches of Saffron Walden and its vicinity* (Saffron Walden: G Youngman, 1845).

Reed, J., 'St Mary's, Saffron Walden Burial Registers 1558-1892' in *Saffron Walden Historical Journal* (Saffron Walden, 2002).

Rowntree, C. B., *Saffron Walden then and now* (Chelmsford: Tindal Press, 1951).

Stacey, H. C., *Saffron Walden in old photographs* (Saffron Walden: The C.W. Daniel Company Limited: 1980).

Uttlesford District Council, *Audley End Conservation Area Appraisal and Draft Management Proposals* (Uttlesford, 2014).

Uttlesford District Council, *Great Chesterford Conservation Area Appraisal and Draft Management Proposals* (Uttlesford, 2007).

Uttlesford District Council, *Littlebury Parish Plan* (Uttlesford, 2009).

Uttlesford District Council, *Littlebury Conservation Area Appraisal and Draft Management Proposals* (Uttlesford, 2011).

Uttlesford District Council, *Saffron Walden Conservation Area Appraisal and Management Proposals* (Uttlesford, 2012).

Uttlesford District Council, *Wendens Ambo Conservation Area Appraisal and Management Proposals* (Uttlesford, 2013).

Valentine, I., *Station 43: Audley End House and SOE's Polish Section* (Stroud: The History Press, 2006).

White, M., *Saffron Walden's history: A chronological compilation* (Saffron Walden: Hart Talbot, 1991).

Websites (all accessed May 2015)

British Library *The British Newspaper Archive,* http://www.britishnewspaperarchive.co.uk/

Essex Record Office, *Saffron Walden 1758,* http://www.essexrecordofficeblog.co.uk/saffron-walden-1758/

Goodge, M., *British Listed Buildings,* http://www.britishlistedbuildings.co.uk

Hunter, I and Wilding, K, *Essex pub history,* http://pubshistory.com/EssexPubs/pubindex.shtml

Littlebury Parish Council, *Littlebury,* http://www.littleburyparishcouncil.org.uk/

Palmer, J.J.N. and Slater, G., *Open Domesday,* http://www.domesdaymap.co.uk/

George, P., *History House: Essex A-Z,* http://www.historyhouse.co.uk/

Recorders of Uttlesford History, *Saffron Walden,* http://www.recordinguttlesfordhistory.org.uk/saffronwalden/saffronwaldenhomepage.html

Saffron Walden Historical Society, *Saffron Walden,* http://saffronwaldenhistory.org.uk/

St Mary's Parish Office, *History of St Mary's Church, Saffron Walden,* http://www.stmaryssaffronwalden.org/

Wendens Ambo Parish Council, *Wendens Ambo,* http://www.wendensambo.org.uk/

Acknowledgements and notes

I would like to thank the readers of my blog, www.essexvoicespast.com, and my connections on Twitter at @EssexVoicesPast who have encouraged me throughout my time writing this book. I am also grateful for the various postcards, photos and memories given to me from members of the Facebook page *Saffron Walden Blast from the Past.* I would also like to thank Jane Fairweather, Jean Harrison and Robina Veal for allowing me to use photographs and postcards from their own personal collections.

Dates attributed to postcards are based on postmarks and/or dates the photographers were active and/or serial numbers on the postcards. Postmarks can only ever be a rough estimate of the date of the postcard; sometimes people purchased postcards but used them many years later, or shops kept old stock for many years. Therefore postmarks are only ever the last possible date of that postcard's view.

Every attempt has been made to seek permission for copyright material used in this book. However, if we have inadvertently used copyright material without permission/ acknowledgement we apologise and we will make the necessary correction at the first opportunity.